Your Guide To The
UNDERWATER WORLD
SYDNEY & THE HARBOUR

I0417547

Steve Hulme

Thanks to Dive Centre Manly for making so many people aware of the underwater world. Without them, and others like them, we would be oblivious to the wonders beneath the waves on our doorsteps.

T: 02 9977 4355
info@divesydney.com.au
www.divesydney.com.au

Published in Australia by Hulmerus Enterprises 2011
Design by Steve Hulme
email: hulmerus@iinet.net.au

Your Guide To The

UNDERWATER WORLD

SYDNEY & THE HARBOUR

The world knows Sydney for its amazing harbour, the bridge and the Opera House. But how many people actually know what beauty and fascination lies beneath the blanket of blue and green they see and travel over every day.

This book, with its pictures supplied by local photographers, gives you a small insight into the wonderful, often weird looking creatures that we as divers and snorkelers see every time we venture under the waves.

If you are a diver you can use this book to help identify some of the wondrous animals you may encounter each time you go diving. They are in alphabetical order for ease of reference. The 'Notes' sections on each page can help you record your sightings and can be an excellent partner to your dive log books.

You may also be happy to know that 5% of the profits from the sale of this book will be going to Project AWARE to help underwater conservation and education around the world.

www.projectaware.org

Ten Ways a Diver Can Protect the Underwater Environment

1. **Dive carefully to protect fragile aquatic ecosystems**
   Many aquatic organisms are delicate and can be harmed by the bump of a camera, the swipe of a fin or even the gentle touch of a hand. Some aquatic organisms like corals grow very slowly and breaking even a small piece can destroy decades of growth. By being careful you can prevent long-term damage to magnificent dive sites.

2. **Be aware of your body and equipment placement when diving**
   Keep your gauges and alternate air source secured so they don't drag over the reef or other vital habitat. Control your buoyancy, taking care not to touch fragile organisms with your body or equipment. You can do your part and prevent injury to aquatic life every time you dive.

3. **Keep your dive skills sharp through continuing education**
   Before heading to open water seek bottom time with a certified professional in a pool or other environment that won't be damaged. You can also refresh your skills and knowledge with a PADI Scuba Review, PADI Advanced Open Water Diver course or Project AWARE Specialty course such as Peak Performance Buoyancy.

4. **Consider how your interactions affect aquatic life**
   Avoid touching, handling, feeding or riding on aquatic life. These actions may stress the animal, interrupt feeding and mating behavior or provoke aggressive behavior in normally nonaggressive species.

5. **Understand and respect underwater life**
   Playing with animals or using them as food for other species can leave a trail of destruction, disrupt local ecosystems and rob other divers of their experiences with these creatures. Consider enrolling in a PADI Underwater Naturalist, AWARE Fish Identification or Coral Reef Conservation Specialty course to better understand sustainable interactions.

6. **Be an ecotourist**
   Make informed decisions when selecting a destination and choose Project AWARE Environmental Operators or other facilities dedicated to sustainable business practices. Obey all local laws and regulations and understand your effect on the environment. Don't collect souvenirs like corals or shells. Instead, take underwater photos and follow Project AWARE's *10 Tips for Underwater Photographers.*

7. **Respect underwater cultural heritage**
   Divers are privileged to access dive sites that are part of our cultural heritage and maritime history. Wrecks can also serve as important habitats for fish and other aquatic life. Help preserve these sites for future generations by obeying local laws, diving responsibly and treating wrecks with respect.

8. **Report environmental disturbances or destruction**
   As a diver, you're in a unique position to monitor the health of local waters. If you notice unusual depletion of aquatic life, injury to aquatic animals or strange substances in the water, report these observations to responsible authorities in your area.

9. **Be a role model for other divers and nondivers when interacting with the environment**
   As a diver, you see the underwater results of carelessness and neglect. Set a good example in your own interactions so that others can learn from you.

10. **Get involved in local environmental activities and issues**
    You can greatly affect your corner of the planet. There are plenty of opportunities to support healthy aquatic environments including Project AWARE conservation and data collection activities like local beach and underwater cleanups and CoralWatch monitoring, supporting environmental legislative issues, attending public hearings on local water resources, conserving water or making responsible seafood choices.

www.projectaware.org

Biscuit Seastar

A small but striking seastar, often seen on
boat dives in and out of the harbour.

Notes: ....
....
....
....

Blackfish or Luderick

You'll find these guys in schools around rocks and patches of kelp. Often seen at the beginning of a shore dive.

Notes: ....
....
....
....

Blenny

Blenny's come in many different guises. Living close to the bottom for protection. Old discarded bottles make great homes

for them. Try not to disturb them on clean up days.

Notes: ....

....

....

....

....

....

Blue Groper

The friendliest of fish.
The big blues are the very territorial males.
All born female, the dominant Groper turns
        male until he dies and is superseded by the
                next largest female who in turn
                becomes male.

Notes: ....
....
....

Blue Morwong

Growing quite a bit bigger than their red cousins. Often being tailed by a group of bream in the multitude of bays around Sydney.

Notes: ....
....
....

Bream

You can't miss these busy fish whenever you go shore diving in Sydney. Whether in half a meter or 10 meters they are always around.

Notes: ....
....
....
....

Bullseyes

Gatherings of Bullseyes can always be found
in and around swim through's. Maybe
the size of their eyes makes
them more comfortable in the
shadows.

Notes: ....
....

'Gunthers' Butterflyfish

These colourful fish are mostly tropical but can be found in Sydney's shallower waters. This little guy is only about 30cm across.

Notes: ....
....
....

Cardinal Fish

These stripey fellows are common around the bays of Sydney. Always digging in the sand, in small schools for tastey morsals.

Notes: ....

....

....

Cockatoo Fish

Cockatoo fish can be found on a rock or
   two. They seem to like lazing around until
   disturbed by a nosey diver or two.

Notes: ....

....

....

....

....

Cowfish

A member of the Boxfish family,
Cowfish have little horns making them
look just like cows!
In a fishy kind of way.

Notes: ....
....
....
....

Crimson Banded Wrasse

A very coulourful fish. At least the male is,
as is often found in the animal kingdom. A
curious guy who'll turn up with his mates
the Maori, Mado & Groper for a
free morsal or two from under
the sand.

Notes: ....

....

Cuttlefish

These cute little critters belong to the same family as octopus and squid. They have an amazing ability to change colour according to their mood. Often found in pairs unlike their larger, solitary cousins the Giant Cuttlefish.

Notes: ....

....

....

Diver (Chris)

You'll often see this unique species hovering around the sea bed. They carry their own air supply while having a great time underwater.

Notes: ....

....

....

Dusky Whaler (juvenile)

These juvenile Dusky's can be found in Cabbage Tree Bay around Fairy Bower. They are only about 1m in length at this age, compared to their 3m parents. Very timid, but if the viz is good, quite easy to spot.

Notes: ....

....

Eagle Ray

See the Eagle Ray literaly fly through the water. Not very commen but quite often seen in the bays of Sydney by divers and snorkelers.

Notes: ....
....
....
....
....

Eastern Pomfred

Not the stripey Mado in front but the mass of silver fish with yellow fins and tails. They school in very large numbers close to shore.

Notes: ....

....

....

....

Eastern Wirrah Cod

A fairly elusive fish. Quite timid but can be found in coastal bays and in the harbour too.

Notes: ....
....
....
....

Feather Duster Worm

The white feathery food gatherers inbetween
the urchin and shrimp filter food down to
the worms stomach, inside a tube in the
rock. Get too close and they'll
disappear inside for protection.

Notes: ....
....
....

Fiddler Ray

Fiddler or Banjo Rays look like the missing
link between sharks and rays. Not surprising
as they are all members of the shark
family.

Notes: ....
....
....
....

Flathead

Flat head, flat body and excellent camouflage
make it very easy to swim past these guys.
Unless they get spooked and dart away
with a quick flick of the tail.

Notes: ....
....
....
....

Giant Cuttlefish

These enigmatic creatures are fantastic to watch as they give colourful displays and make various gestures with their arms. Usually telling you to 'GO AWAY, I'm busy!'

Notes: ....

....

....

....

Girdled Scallyfin

A common damsel fish around the coast
and in the harbour of Sydney.

Notes: ....
....
....
....

Gloomy Octopus

Look for clusters of shells around a hole in
the sand and you'll most likely see a pair
of eyes peering back at you. Wiggle your
fingers so they look like little fish, in
front of the hole and prepare for
a long, curious tentacle to greet
you, looking for lunch.

Notes: ....
....

Goatfish

With their goat like barbels on their chin, goatfish are constantly searching for food among the sand.

Notes: ....
....
....
....

Goby

There are many types of Goby. This little guy is very well adapted to darting around the seabed.

Notes: ....
....
....
....

Half Striped Perch

The colours on the Perch make it ideal to live among the colourful sponge's and soft corals of Sydney.

Notes: ....
....
....
....

Hermit Crabs

Hermits crabs are found in their thousands
across the bays of New South Wales.   Cast
off shells are abundant for the crabs
needing new homes as they grow.
Notes: ....
....
....
....
....

Herring Cale

Dark blue males and orange females swim
in and out of the thick kelp. Very quick
and agile, quite a feet to get a
photo in focus!

Notes: ....

....

....

Hulafish

Always in small or big schools for
protection. Hulafish are one of the most
common smaller fish around
Sydney .

Notes: ....
....
....

Immaculate Damselfish

These damsel fish have beautiful blue
iridescent fins and tails. Sometimes alone
on the reef or in larger schools
out deep.

Notes: ....
....
....

Large tooth Beardy

Always hidden under rocks and in crevices.
Beardies are fairly common in the harbour
and ocean side and will always be found
in the same spot.

Notes: ....
....
....
....

Leatherjackets - Black Reef

Black Reef Leatherjackets can always be
found on a boat dive, usually in pairs.
But don't be surprised to see
them closer to shore.

Notes: ....
....
....

Leatherjackets - Pigmy

At only a fraction of the size of their cousins, these cute little Leatherjackets can be found hiding under kelp.

Notes: ....
....
....
....

Leatherjacket – Six Spine

Six Spine Leatherjackets are frequently seen grazing on the seagrass at Cabbage Tree Bay.

Notes: ....
....
....
....

Lionfish

Sydney quite often gets visited by some of the more tropical creatures of the ocean. Lionfish with their extremely venomous fins are one such visitor.

Notes: ....

....

Long Nose Boarfish

Boarfish are at home in the harbour or out at depth. They make a novel change to the usual suspects on a dive.

Notes: ....
....
....
....

Mado

Mado scurry around for scraps, following divers with buoyancy issues kicking up the sand.

Notes: ....
....
....
....

Maori Wrasse

Ever looked behind you on a dive? You're sure to see a Maori or two following you around waiting for a fin to kick up the sand & release some tasty morsels. Like birds cracking shells on rocks these guys do the same with snails. Very clever fish!

Notes: ....
....
....

Green Moray Eel

Don't tempt these short sighted eels with a
finger. They'll think it's a tasty treat to eat!

Notes: ....
....
....
....
....
....

Motor Bike

There are many wrecks in the world, but the motor bike at Shelly Beach in Manly is one that prevokes questions as to how and why? But is a great find and full of life.

Notes: ....
....
....

Mullet

These guys were found schooling in the
shallows. A fish found worldwide but
imortalised in Australia for being in the
saying "like a stunned mullet",
belwidered or astonished.

Notes: ....

....

....

Nudibranch

Gastropods - slugs & snails.
Latin:
Nudi - meaning naked, without shell.
Branch - meaning Gills.
Extremely popular with macro
photographers.

Notes: ....
....
....

Obese Sea Pen

Sea Pens come out to feed at night. Often mistaken for plants, they use their leaf like body parts to trap food floating by.

Notes: ....

....

....

Old Wives

Endemic to Australia, Old Wives are a
wondrous fish to come across. Especially
when you encounter them in
large schools.

Notes: ....
....
....

Pike

Ever present on shore dives. Watch out for them swimming around you on a night dive. A silver flash darts in to get some prey lit up by your torch.

Notes: ....
....
....

Red Morwong

Very common in Sydney waters. Find Red Morwong sitting on rocks or under kelp.

Notes: ....
....
....
....
....

Rock Cod

Member of the scorpionfish family, the Rock Cod can grow quite large in size. When you approach them, their dorsal fins fan up to reveal venomous spines. Not deadly like their cousins the Stonefish, but painful enough to give them plenty of respect!

Notes: ....

....

Sawtail

Easy to identify by several black spots coming from the tail.

Notes: ....
....
....
....
....

Sea Anemone

Most spectacular at night, when anemone's
come out to feed with all the other weird
and wonderful creatures.

Notes: ....
....
....
....

Seahorse

Captivating their audience. You can find these
small critters hanging off any shark nets at
the beach or around piers and boardwalks
in the Harbour.

Notes: ....
....
....
....

Senator Wrasse

A striking green fish with various other
colours dotted throughout it's body.
Often found hiding in the kelp.

Notes: ....
....
....
....

Sergeant Baker

Like lizards sitting on rocks, Sergeant Bakers
are named after Governor Phillip's
sergeant, who was probably the first
white settler to catch one.

Notes: ....
....
....
....

Shrimp

Can you see it? They can see you. They move so fast when you get close. On a night dive look out for the hundreds of red eyes watching you from under the rocks.

Notes: ....

....

....

....

Shovel Nose Ray

The Shovel Nose Ray is also a relative of
the shark but its habits are more
that of a ray.

Notes: ....

....

....

Snowy Vollute

Very large seasnail. Usually buried under
the sand by day, but out and about at
night searching for food.

Notes: ....
....
....
....

Sting Ray

Very common all around Sydney and the harbour. Look for a pair of eyes poking out of the sand, waiting for their prey.

Notes: ....

....

....

....

....

Stripey

These fish certainly live up to their name with a vivid yellow and black pattern. Found mostly in protected bays and in the harbour.

Notes: ....
....
....
....

Urchins

Animals in their own right, NOT for luring groper, urchins crawl out of their cover at night to feed. Where there maybe 2 or 3 in the day, there can be hundreds at night.

Notes: ....
....
....

Weedy Seadragon

This strange looking fellow is probably Sydney's most sought after sighting. About 40cm in length they are hard to spot among the kelp. In this photo you can see the eggs on the tail of the male seadragon. As with their cousins the seahorses, the male is the one who incubates the eggs until they hatch

Notes: ....

....

White Ears

Named for the white patch by the gills. The juvenilles are born gold with electric blue markings. They grow up to lose their colour for complete grey.

Notes: ....
....
....
....

White Trevally

Juvenilles pictured here. White Trevally can
be identified by the black dot by the gills
and the juvenilles by the yellow
stripe across the body.

Notes: ....

....

....

Wobbegong Shark

Wobby's can grow up to 3m in length. Look under ledges during the day to spot these sleepy animals. But at night they are out on the sand, eyes like cats eyes in the torch light. Don't pull their tails! They are the only shark that can bite their own tail (if they wanted to).

Notes: ....
....
....

Yellow Tail

A very common schooling fish. In and around the shallows or deeper down, but always in large numbers. Great for swimming through and out the other side.

Notes: ....
....
....

Marine Debris - the facts

6 million tonnes of debris enter the oceans each year

Did you know?

- Marine debris in the world's oceans causes harm to underwater environments and wildlife.

- In 2008, 10,600 divers removed 219,528 lbs (99.57 tons) of debris from over 1,000 miles of underwater terrain, an average of 25 pounds per diver.

- One million plastic bags are used every minute of the day and almost three million tons of plastic are used to bottle water globally every year.

- Toxic chemicals in the 4.5 trillion cigarette filters littered worldwide every year threatens the wellbeing of marine life.

- Nearly 80 percent of all marine debris is plastic. In some parts of the ocean plastic outweighs plankton 6:1.

- An estimated 46,000 pieces of plastic litter alone are floating on every square mile of ocean, 70 percent of which will eventually sink.

- Plastics do not biodegrade. When plastic debris meets water it remains for centuries, breaking down slowly into smaller fragments and finally into plastic dust.

- Aluminum cans take up to 100 years to degrade and 6-pack holder rings 450 years.

- It takes glass bottles one million years to biodegrade in the natural environment.

- Entanglement and ingestion of fishing line, nets, rope and other debris has been reported in more than 260 animal species worldwide.

- An estimated 100,000 marine mammals including dolphins, whales, seals and sea turtles choke or get tangled in debris every year. And 86 percent of all sea turtles are affected by marine debris.

- More than 1 million seabirds are killed by litter each year.

Tips to keep waters debris free

1) Remove debris on every recreational dive or shoreline visit.

2) The number one item found in cleanups is cigarette filters. Always dispose of them properly and never overboard.

3) Reduce, reuse and recycle.

4) Avoid buying plastic products.

5) Be aware of everything you buy and avoid excessive packaging.

6) Demand improved and increased number of recycling facilities for your area.

7) Properly dispose of all pieces of fishing line, net or other associated litter.

8) Keep plastics and rubbish off the ground and the ocean floor.

9) Keep storm drains and shorelines free of rubbish.

10) Get involved in Project AWARE shoreline and underwater cleanups year-round or during September's International Cleanup Day.

www.projectaware.org

The Decomposition Rate of Marine Debris

Glass Bottle - 1 million years

Monofilament fishing line - 600 years

Plastic beverage bottles - 450 years

Disposable diapers - 450 years

Aluminium can - 80-200 years

Foamed plastic buoy - 80 years

Rubber boat sole - 50-80 years

Foamed plastic cup - 50 years

Tin can - 50 years

Leather - 50 years

Nylon Fabric - 30-40 years

Plastic film canister - 20-30 years

Plastic Bag - 10-20 years

Cigarette filter - 1-50 years

Wool sock - 1-5 years

Plywood - 1-3 years

Waxed milk carton - 3 months

Apple core - 2 months

Newspaper - 6 weeks

Orange or banana peel - 2-5 weeks

Paper towel - 2-4 weeks

Courtesy of Wolcott Henry

"From Pocket Guide... to Marine Debris," The Ocean Conservancy, 2004.
Sources: U.S National Park Service; Mote Marine Lab, FL and "Garbage In, Garbage Out"

www.ingramcontent.com/pod-product-compliance
Lightning Source LLC
Chambersburg PA
CBHW050811290526
45792CB00001B/69

* 9 7 8 1 4 5 3 8 5 3 8 9 4 *